Donated by
The Friends of the Library
2001

INSIDER'S GUIDE TO THE BODY

The Immune System

Susie Derkins

the rosen publishing group's
**rosen
central**

Published in 2001 by The Rosen Publishing Group, Inc.
29 East 21st Street, New York, NY 10010

First Edition

Library of Congress Cataloging in Publication Data

Derkins, Susie.
     The immune system / by Susie Derkins.
          p.   cm. — (The insider's guide to the body)
Includes bibliographical references and index.
     ISBN 0-8239-3339-3 (lib. bdg. : alk. paper)
   1. Immune system—Juvenile literature. [1. Immune system.] I. Title. II. Series.
     QR181.8 .D474 2000
     616.07'9—dc21

                                                                00-010216

Manufactured in the United States of America

Contents

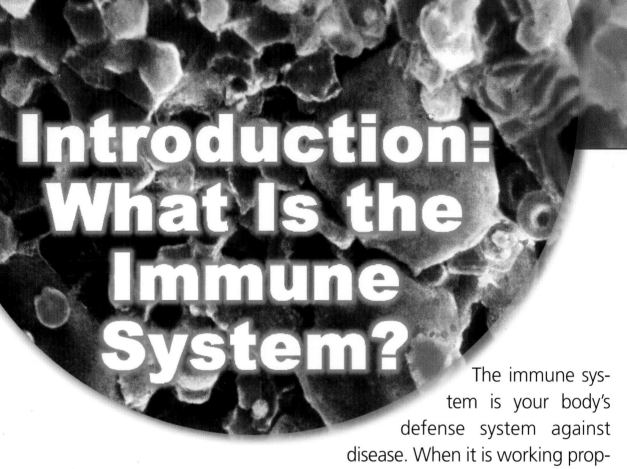

Introduction: What Is the Immune System?

The immune system is your body's defense system against disease. When it is working properly, it finds and fights pathogenic, or disease-causing, organisms like germs, bacteria, and viruses. Your immune system gives you the physical and mental strength, energy, and power to fight minor illnesses such as colds or flu. A healthy immune system can also detect and repair damaged cells, such as ones that have been injured by cancer and other diseases.

But when your immune system is weakened, serious problems can occur. You may experience frequent or long-lasting infections—ones that reoccur over months or won't go away at all. An unwell immune system may fail to detect unhealthy cell growth, resulting in cancers that cannot be fought off by the body alone. This means that you may have to seek other therapies, such as chemotherapy or radiation therapy, to complete the job of fighting disease.

Almost all major diseases, including cancer, heart disease, and AIDS, are the result of an unhealthy or damaged immune system.

Even health problems that are not a direct result of an immune system malfunction, such as a broken bone or genetic defect, cannot be healed or controlled unless a person's immune system is strong and healthy.

One way to understand how the immune system works is to think of what happens to a living creature when it dies. If you have ever seen a dead animal, perhaps a squirrel or rabbit that has been struck by a car, you may have noticed how the creature's body immediately shuts down and becomes stiff. Within hours, the animal's body is invaded by parasites and microscopic bacteria. This is because when an animal is alive, its immune system can fight off infection. Once the immune system stops working, all types of foreign invaders take apart the bodily organs and tissues. Eventually, the bacteria and parasites will eat away at all of the animal's body parts, leaving behind just a skeleton.

This book will explain to you how your immune system works to keep you healthy and fight infection, tell you about the major types of immune system diseases and how they are commonly treated, and give you lots of information about how to keep your own immune system working at its best. Your immune system is your body's way of defending your health and keeping you alive, so it's important to understand how it works.

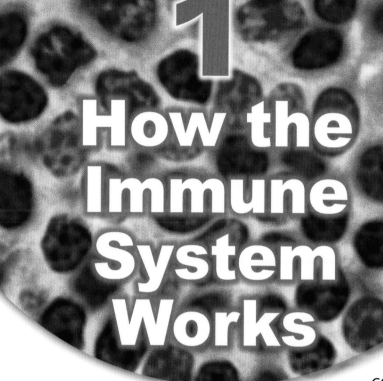

1

How the Immune System Works

Your body's immune system is a very complicated network of organs and cells that work together to fight deadly intruders called antigens, which are any organism that could make you sick, like bacteria, microbes, parasites, and viruses. An antigen, such as a virus, is a parasite. A parasite cannot survive by itself—it needs to feed off of an animal, human, or plant (also called the host) to survive. Once inside the cells of a host, a virus tries to become active and multiply. If it is successful, it can eventually create so many copies of itself that it causes the cell to burst, releasing the virus into the body. Then the virus finds more cells in your body in which to live. This process can continue on and on, until the virus has attacked enough cells to make you ill. However, a healthy and strong immune system can usually kill any viruses before they multiply to such a damaging degree.

Organs of the Immune System

The immune system consists of the thymus, bone marrow, spleen, and lymph nodes. All of these components must function together in order to keep your body strong and ready to fight infection. If one of these components is ill or weakened and cannot do its infection-fighting job, the other parts will not work well either.

Thymus

The thymus gland is the master gland of the immune system. Its job is to produce T cells, the cells responsible for fighting disease. The thymus is located in the thorax, the body cavity between the

This is a false-color electron micrograph of the cortex, or outer part, of the thymus. The thymus produces T cells (the yellow spheres) which fight disease.

neck and the abdomen that also houses the heart and lungs. The thymus is extremely important early in a person's life. Sometimes, a baby will be born without a thymus, causing the immune system to collapse and the baby to die. However, the thymus of an adult can usually be removed without such deadly results. This is because an adult's immune system is stronger and more mature, and the other organs can handle the immune system's functions.

Bone Marrow

The bone marrow produces both red blood cells, which carry oxygen throughout the body, and white blood cells, which destroy

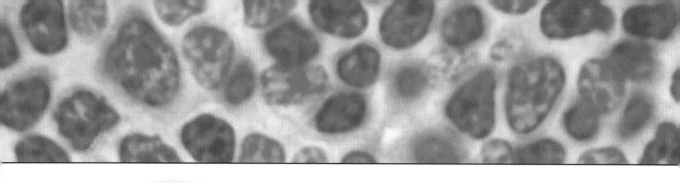

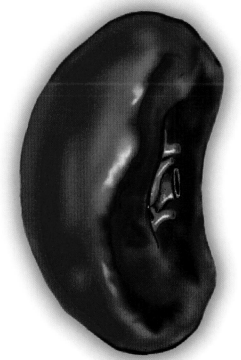

The spleen is an organ located in the abdomen that filters antigens out of the blood.

bacteria. It produces these cells through a process called hematopoiesis. The bone marrow produces B cells and "natural killer" cells. (All of these types of cells are described a little later in this chapter.)

Spleen

The spleen acts as the immune system's cleaning agent. It filters antigens out of the blood. It is located on the upper left side of the abdomen. It is made up of macrophages and dendritic cells, as well as B cells, T cells, natural killer cells, and red blood cells. Macrophages and dendritic cells migrate, or travel, through the blood, seek out antigens in your system, and carry them back to the spleen. Once the antigens are in the spleen, the appropriate B cells or T cells begin an "immune response"—they fight infection by producing antibodies. Antibodies are special proteins that recognize and attach themselves to a specific antigen. They then tell other cells to surround and kill or remove that substance from the body. The spleen is also responsible for destroying old red blood cells that are no longer useful.

Lymph Nodes

The lymph nodes also act as filters for the body's infection-fighting system. They are small and bean-shaped, and are clustered in certain areas of the body such as the neck, groin, and under the arm. Made up mostly of T cells, B cells, dendritic cells, and macrophages, the lymph nodes use a bodily fluid called lymph to drain fluid from the

Bone marrow produces red blood cells (the orange disc shapes above) and white blood cells (the pale spheres in the lower center).

body's tissues. Antigens are filtered out of lymph in the lymph nodes, then the lymph is recirculated throughout the body. The lymph nodes function much the same way the spleen does, as macrophages and dendritic cells carry antigens to the B cells or T cells of the lymph nodes, initiating an immune response and producing antibodies.

Cells of the Immune System

The cells of the immune system are red blood cells—which keep your blood flowing properly and carry oxygen throughout the body—and

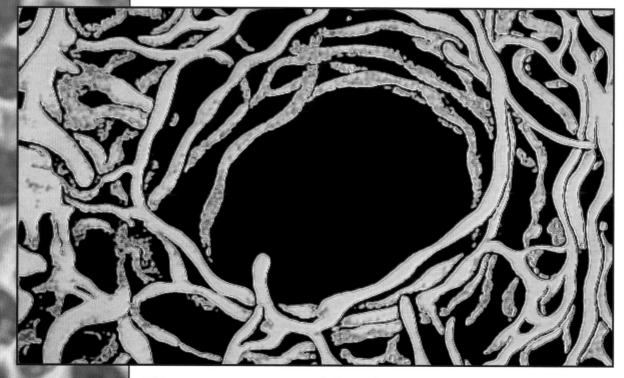

This cross section view of the spleen shows a network of fibers called trabeculae surrounding a round nodule containing white blood cells.

white blood cells—which are responsible for starting an immune response. Red blood cells contain hemoglobin, a complex protein substance that allows oxygen to be distributed throughout the bloodstream. White blood cells, also known as leukocytes, are actually a collection of many different types of cells which are essential to make the immune system work. The most important white blood cells of the immune system are described in the following pages.

T Cells

T cells are the cells responsible for immunity or disease resistance. There are two major types of T cells:

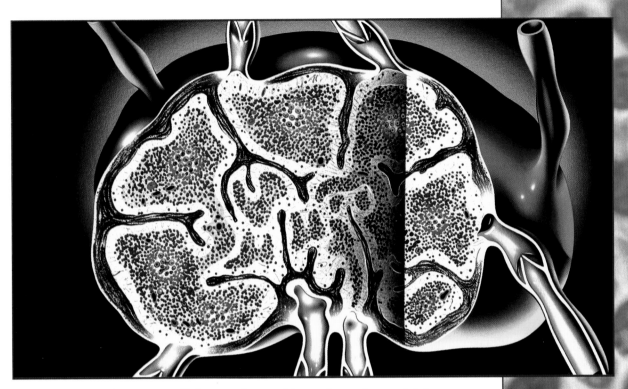

Like the spleen, small bean-shaped lymph nodes, which occur in clusters throughout the body, act as filters for the body's infection-fighting system.

T helpers, and T killers or suppressors. The main function of T helper cells is to make the body's immune system stronger by alerting other types of white blood cells to the presence of an antigen. They do this by producing special chemicals or secretions which tell the other cells to fight.

T killers, on the other hand, are responsible for directly killing certain tumor cells, virus-infected cells, and parasites. T killers must be alerted by the helper cells to start an attack. If T cells are attacked by a virus that cannot be killed quickly enough, such as HIV, the entire body is left open for a deadly disease like AIDS. Both types of T cells are made in your bone marrow and develop in the thymus. They fight infection in the lymph nodes and the spleen.

B Cells

The main function of B cells is the production of antibodies in response to antigens such as bacteria, viruses, and tumor cells. Antibodies recognize viral substances in the body and bind themselves to them, sending a signal to other cells to surround and kill the illness-causing substance. These cells, like T cells, originate in the bone marrow.

Natural Killer Cells

Natural killer or NK cells are much like T killer cells. They directly kill tumors such as melanomas and lymphomas, as well as cells infected by viruses. Unlike T killers though, NK cells kill their targets directly without first needing to be told by T helpers. However, when NK cells are told to fight by the secretions given off by T helper cells, they can kill tumors and viruses even more effectively.

Macrophages

Macrophages regulate the immune system's responses. These cells take the important step of starting the immune response. They act as scavengers, picking up and consuming antigens and bringing them to other cells, such as T cells or B cells. Then the

Macrophages travel through the blood, consuming antigens and bringing them to the spleen, where an immune response begins.

T cells and B cells begin their attack and attempt to kill the infectious material.

Dendritic Cells

Dendritic cells originate in the bone marrow. Much like macrophages, they capture antigens. But instead of taking them to T cells and B cells, they deliver them directly to the thymus, lymph nodes, and spleen. Dendritic cells can also be found in the bloodstream and bodily tissues. Medical researchers have paid a lot of attention to dendritic cells in recent years because it is believed that they bind high amounts of the HIV

Antibodies are Y-shaped cells produced by white blood cells that bind to antigens and deliver them to T cells and B cells to be destroyed.

virus. Researchers think that these cells may be responsible for transmitting HIV to T cells in order to activate an immune response.

The Immune
System Response

The immune system's white blood cells produce antibodies. Antibodies are Y-shaped. The tips of each of the two branches of the Y are sensitive to specific antigens. That means that a certain antigen will stick to an antibody's tips, binding it to that antibody. A large number of antibodies can bind to one antigen and deliver it to a T cell or B cell. Then the T cells or B cells proliferate, or multiply, alerting the rest of the immune system that the antigen needs to be destroyed.

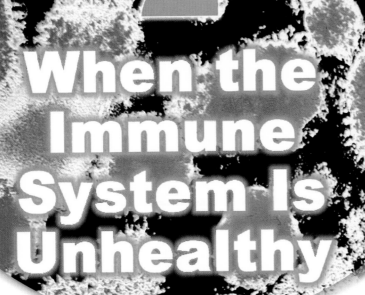

2

When the Immune System Is Unhealthy

A compromised, or endangered, immune system can lead to temporary conditions such as colds, fevers, hives, and inflammation. But it can also invite far more serious and even deadly diseases, such as cancer and AIDS. The good news, however, is that many disorders of the immune system are controllable—if not completely avoidable—if you eat well and make healthy lifestyle choices. For the most part, you have a lot of control over the health of your immune system.

How Diseases Affect the Immune System

When you get sick, your body cannot work at its full potential. Sometimes your immune system cannot keep up with the levels of bacteria that have entered your system. When this happens, you show symptoms, or signs of illness, such as feeling overly tired or nauseous. Some types of infection are far more serious than others. Let's take a look at some of the most common types of immune system diseases.

Colds and Influenza

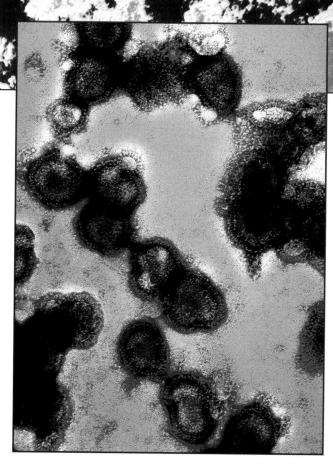

The reason why you often hear the expression "the common cold" is because cold viruses attack nearly everyone at some point, and because colds can be caused by over 200 different viruses. Kids—especially young ones—are at special risk for cold viruses because crowded classrooms and school buses are places where the virus is easily passed from one person to another. Colds, characterized by sneezing, runny nose, coughing, and fatigue, are annoying but basically harmless. The only known cure is time—and plenty of fluids and rest.

Influenza, or the flu, is very common and very contagious. A dead or weak form of the virus is used as a vaccine, stimulating the immune system to make antibodies to fight off the flu.

Likewise, influenza (more commonly known as the flu) is very common and very contagious—it's easy to catch from those around you who are infected. At least 90 million Americans come down with the flu every year! The flu vaccine, usually called a flu shot, can protect people against the flu. It is made from a dead or weak influenza virus and is given to people who haven't yet gotten sick with the flu. When the vaccine is injected into your body, it triggers your immune system

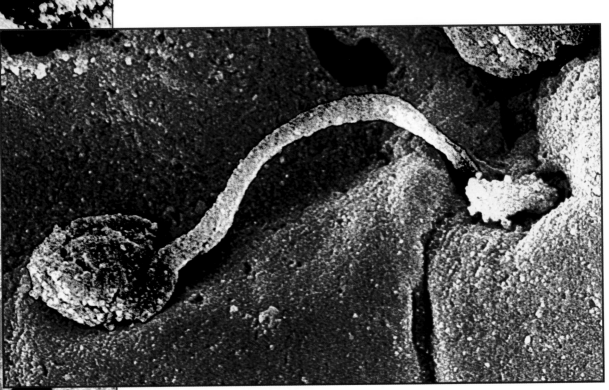

Pneumonia, a disease that infects the lungs, can be very serious. The image above shows a white blood cell probing a diseased lung.

to make antibodies that fight off the flu. Your immune system becomes stronger and more prepared to fight the flu if it should attack your system. Flu shots can reduce the chance of flu infection by 60 to 80 percent.

Pneumonia

Pneumonia, a disease that infects the lungs, affects one in every 100 people each year and can be very dangerous if left untreated. There are different categories of pneumonia, which range in seriousness from mild to life-threatening. People often come down with pneumonia when they have the flu. The pneumonia will usually set in two to three days after initial flu symptoms have started. Common symptoms of pneumonia are coughing up greenish mucus, severe chest pains, fatigue, high fever, chills, nausea, vomiting, and an all-over ache. In severe cases, you may also experience a persistent hacking cough, shortness of breath, coughing up blood, or abdominal pains. Pneumonia can usually be cured by anti-biotic medication. In more serious cases, your lungs may fill with toxic fluids that have to be drained out in the hospital.

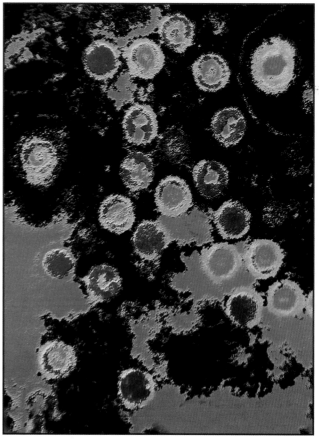

The Epstein-Barr virus is a form of the herpes virus that also causes mononucleosis and chronic fatigue syndrome.

Epstein-Barr Virus and Mononucleosis

Epstein-Barr Virus (EBV) is a form of the herpes virus. The presence of Epstein-Barr virus in the body is confirmed by a blood test. If you have been infected with EBV, a doctor will see an increased number of white blood cells when looking at your blood under a microscope. Studies have shown that most people have been infected with EBV at some point—most without even realizing it because they have few or no symptoms.

Mononucleosis, sometimes just called mono, is related to Epstein-Barr because it is caused by the same virus. It causes the lymph nodes to swell. Other symptoms include sore throat, nausea, headache, loss

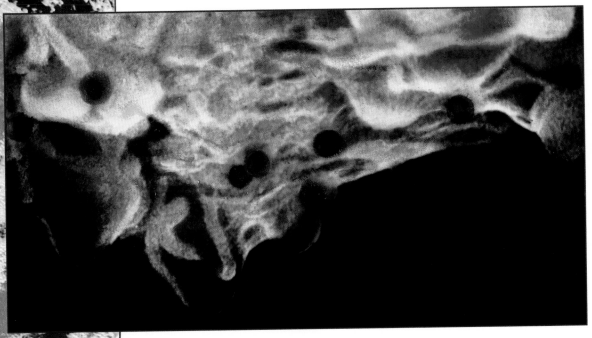

AIDS overwhelms the immune system so seriously that it can no longer function. This image shows the effects of HIV on a T cell.

of appetite, muscle fatigue, and weakness. Mono infection is highly contagious but not very serious (except in rare cases, when it can cause an enlargement and rupturing of the spleen). Bed rest is the most common recommendation for treatment of mono. Chronic fatigue syndrome (CFS) is another variation of the Epstein-Barr virus. People with CFS suffer from a fatigued, weak state that does not go away. They are tired and unable to concentrate for prolonged periods of time—months, and sometimes even years. So far, there is no vaccine for CFS.

AIDS (Acquired Immuno-deficiency Syndrome)

AIDS is short for acquired immunodeficiency syndrome. Acquired means that the disease is contracted; it comes from outside your body. HIV, the virus

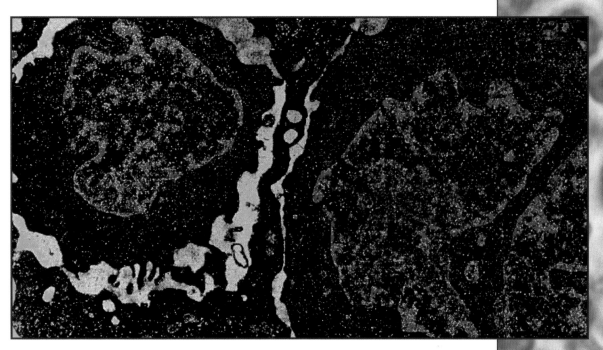

This electron micrograph shows cancer cells that have been engulfed by macrophages.

believed to be responsible for causing AIDS, is passed from an infected person to an uninfected person through certain body fluids. Immunodeficiency, a combination of the words "immune" and "deficiency," means that the immune system is not working properly. "Syndrome" means that there are symptoms of the disease. As of 1995, 20 percent of all AIDS cases were people in their twenties. This means that these people probably contracted the disease as teenagers, because symptoms of AIDS only show up after about ten years.

AIDS overwhelms the body's immune system so severely that it can no longer function properly. The effects of HIV on a person's immune system cause the body to be unable to fight infection, and so the person acquires dangerous diseases, such as pneumonia.

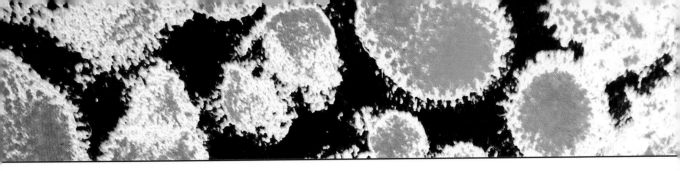

Contracting a disease like pneumonia weakens the immune system even further, and can often lead to a person's immune system shutting down completely, resulting in death.

Cancer

The growth and development of cancer is the result of an increase in the number of abnormal cells in the body caused by cell damage, usually genetic. The growth of these cells, called metastasis, destroys surrounding body tissues and often spreads to other parts of the body. Cancer can develop anywhere in the body, but the organs most commonly attacked by cancer are the lungs, brain, breast, prostate, colon, ovaries, and skin. Unlike AIDS or the flu, cancer is not contracted from outside the body, but develops inside. Therefore, cancer is not contagious.

During metastasis, the rate of abnormal cell growth is so accelerated, or sped up, that the growth of malignant (cancerous) tumors often occurs. Tumors are very dangerous,

Heart disease is the number one cause of death in the United States.

because as they grow, they put pressure on nearby organs and body tissues. Sometimes they grow so big that they invade these nearby organs or tissues, damaging or even disabling them and opening them up to further infection. Not all tumors are cancerous, and the ones that aren't—called benign tumors—can usually be removed without further problems. While some forms of cancer are genetic, it has been proven that factors

This is a cross section of an artery blocked with plaque, a condition known as atherosclerosis.

such as smoking or a high-fat diet can cause certain types of cancer, such as lung or colon cancer. For more information on lifestyle choices and health, see chapter 4.

Heart Disease

Heart disease, the number-one cause of death in America, is a disease characterized by a severe abnormality in the heart and in blood circulation. Healthy arteries—the channels of the circulatory system in which blood flows away from the heart—are flexible and strong, and blood flows easily through them. But when they get clogged with plaque and other fatty deposits, the arteries' narrow channels are putting extra pressure on the heart to pump blood through the body. This condition is known as atherosclerosis—a serious build-up of plaque in the arteries that can lead to high blood pressure, and eventually a heart attack or stroke.

Heart disease is directly linked to certain behavioral choices, such as a high-fat, high-cholesterol diet. Cholesterol is a fatlike substance that protects and insulates cell membranes and helps to create hormones in the body. However, too much cholesterol in the diet is also one of the leading causes of certain types of cancer. A high-fat, high-cholesterol diet is very common in America, where fast food and processed foods are popular. Smoking and alcohol abuse can further damage the arteries, and a lack of physical activity only worsens the condition.

Diabetes

Diabetes is a disease characterized by the body's inability to produce enough of a natural drug called insulin. Insulin is a chemical released by the pancreas to process sugars in the diet. Diabetics must carefully manage their blood sugar levels or risk heart and blood vessel problems. A combination of diet, weight control, exercise, and regular injections of insulin can help to control the condition. While diabetes is strongly linked to heredity, it can also be triggered by increased blood sugar and fat levels—in other words, by a poor diet. And smokers who are diabetic are at extremely serious risk for heart problems such as heart attack or heart failure.

These hexagonal crystals are insulin, a hormone produced by the pancreas to process sugar. Diabetes is a disease characterized by the body's inability to produce insulin.

Other disorders related to the immune system include chemical sensitivity, environmental illnesses, and candida, a parasitic fungal infection. And in some people, the immune system overreacts. This can result in health problems such as allergies or hyperthyroidism, an excessive functioning of the thyroid that can cause extreme weight loss or high blood pressure. A compromised immune system can even attack itself, causing diseases such as lupus or multiple sclerosis. The next chapter will describe the way that immune system disease is most often treated. And chapter 4 will let you know the best methods to prevent immune system disorders—through smart, healthy lifestyle choices.

3

Treating Immune System Disease

There are three conventional ways to treat immune disease. The most common approach is to treat the symptoms. This means that your doctor might prescribe antibiotics to treat an infection, or that you may undergo radiation therapy to treat cancer, or have surgery to remove a tumor. While these methods of treatment can fight the initial infection, they can also suppress parts of the immune system at the same time, leaving the body open to new infections.

Another method of treatment is to suppress an overactive immune system with anti-inflammatory drugs such as ibuprofen or steroids. Although use of these drugs may initially relieve symptoms, this method of treatment can also result in serious side effects and weaken the immune system even further. This leads to more medical problems that are treated with even more drugs. A third method of treatment, one that is far less frequently used, is genetic engineering through techniques that duplicate the body's immune system.

Antibiotics

In some cases, your immune system is unable to activate itself fast enough to fight off antigens. Perhaps bacteria are reproducing so quickly that permanent damage will occur before your immune system is able to kill them. In a situation like this, your doctor will probably prescribe an antibiotic—a chemical that will kill infected cells but not harm other cells in your body.

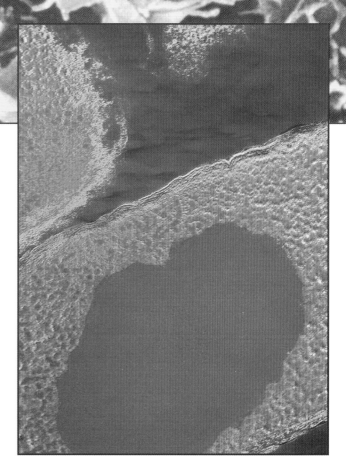

Above is an E. coli bacterium that has been genetically engineered to stimulate the immune system.

An antibiotic works very quickly, usually clearing up the worst symptoms of infection within two or three days. It completely destroys the infection-causing bacteria within a week to ten days. But one problem with antibiotics is that, over time, they can lose their power to work. Bacteria treated with antibiotics sometimes mutate—or change form—and are no longer affected by the antibiotic. The mutated bacteria will then reproduce and start a whole new infection that is immune to the antibiotic you were taking. Doctors and medical researchers are very concerned about mutations, which is one of the main reasons that doctors do not want to overprescribe antibiotic medication to sick patients.

Surgery

Surgery is the oldest method of treating cancer and other tumors and growths. A doctor will surgically remove all or part of an infected organ, or cut a tumor out of the body. Most of the time, part of the tissue surrounding the tumor or cancerous cells will also be removed, in case infection has spread. Surgery is a common method of treatment for cancers of the lung, breast, colon, and mouth. Many times, surgery is a first step in cancer therapy. After the cancerous cells have been cut from the body, a patient will start radiation therapy or chemotherapy.

Radiation Therapy and Chemotherapy

Radiation therapy is the use of X rays to destroy cancer cells. A beam of radioactive light is directed at a cancerous tumor, shrinking or killing it. Radiation therapy—also called radiotherapy, X-ray therapy, or irradiation—is usually used along with other treatments, such as surgery and chemotherapy. Sometimes radiation is used before surgery, to shrink a tumor before it is removed. Other times radiation therapy is used after surgery, to kill any remaining infected cells or tissue. In some cases, such as when it is too dangerous or difficult to perform surgery on a particular area of the body, radiation therapy is the only method of treatment.

Chemotherapy is the use of drugs to kill cancerous cells. It is used much in the same way as radiation therapy, but is especially

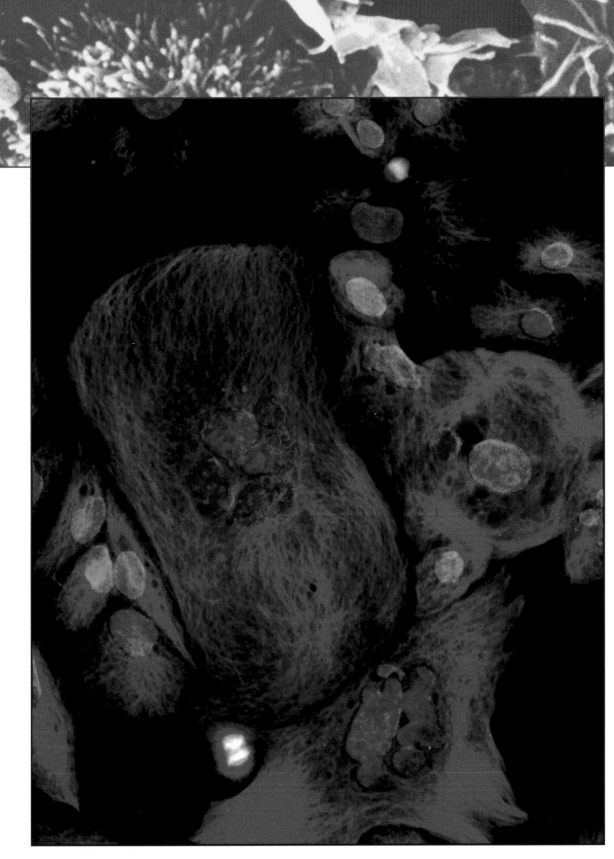

In the image above, the rapid cell division of cancer cells of the human bladder has been stopped with chemotherapy.

helpful in fighting cancer that has spread throughout the body. When cancer cannot be easily detected and hit with a beam of radiation, chemotherapy "blankets" the body with anticancer drugs. There are more than fifty different anticancer drugs commonly used in chemotherapy, and most of them are able to kill cancer cells without doing too much damage to healthy cells. Both radiation therapy and chemotherapy are commonly used to treat cancers of the lung, breast, prostate, testicles, and bladder.

Immunization

There are some viruses that are so dangerous or deadly that it is not always best to give the body's immune system a chance to attack them naturally. Sometimes the smartest thing is to prevent a person from catching it at all through a process called immunization. Immunization is when a person's immune system is activated by a vaccine. Vaccines, like the influenza vaccine mentioned in chapter 2, are made up of dead or weak viruses and are used to activate the immune system. After being vaccinated, your body is able to create a defense mechanism against the disease and you will not be infected by it. You are immune.

Alternative Treatments

Many doctors and other medical experts and researchers are beginning to see the benefits of a more holistic, or whole-bodied, approach to the treatment of disease. This is because doctors know

that proper nutrition, exercise, deep sleep, and a positive psychological state can all dramatically affect the immune system. Holistically oriented treatment attempts to gently correct imbalances in the body by letting the body naturally restore its immune functions. Doctors who practice holistic medicine try to treat a patient's entire body, not just the part that is diseased.

Homeopathy has also become very popular in the treatment of immune disease. Homeopathy is a medical practice that works on the principle of the "law of similarity," which says: A substance that causes the same symptoms as the illness a sick person is fighting, taken in very small doses, can heal those symptoms. In other words, homeopathy works by attacking a symptom with that symptom.

The type of treatment that a doctor will seek for his or her patients depends on many things, such as the particular immune disease, the patient's age, and the physical health of the patient at the time of infection. No one method of treatment is best for everyone, so it is important for people—especially those who have very serious immune system problems such as AIDS or cancer—to do plenty of research. If you or someone you know is suffering from an immune system disorder, find out the facts on the different treatment options. Talk to several different doctors and other health experts to find out what kinds of methods and approaches exist. Most important, try to speak with people who have had the immune system disorder that you are dealing with, so that you can get firsthand accounts of what different methods of therapy are really like.

4

How to Stay Healthy and Strong

There are many things that you can do to keep yourself in good physical condition and prevent disease. The most important elements of preventative health are a proper diet, regular exercise, and plenty of rest. What you eat is especially significant when it comes to your immune system. Read on for more information about what is needed for a healthy diet.

Good Things

● **Protein.** Protein is an important nutrient for strong muscles and sustained energy. Most people know that chicken and fish are sources of protein that are lower in saturated fat and cholesterol than beef or pork. However, many nutritionists advocate nonanimal sources of protein. This is because foods such as beans, nuts, and soy products are completely free of saturated fats and artery-clogging cholesterol. They also contain substances called antioxidants, which many doctors believe help to prevent cancer. Good sources of protein include tofu, whole grains such as brown rice, and dark green vegetables such as spinach, kale, and broccoli.

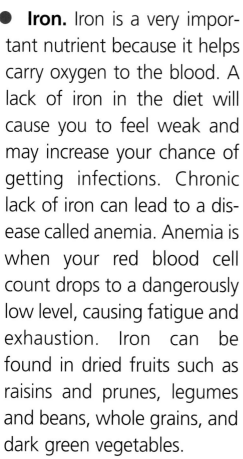

- **Iron.** Iron is a very important nutrient because it helps carry oxygen to the blood. A lack of iron in the diet will cause you to feel weak and may increase your chance of getting infections. Chronic lack of iron can lead to a disease called anemia. Anemia is when your red blood cell count drops to a dangerously low level, causing fatigue and exhaustion. Iron can be found in dried fruits such as raisins and prunes, legumes and beans, whole grains, and dark green vegetables.

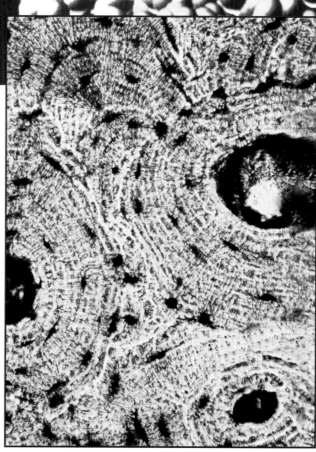

Bones are made up primarily of calcium. In this close-up view of a compact bone, narrow spaces are visible between hard, calcified connective tissue.

- **Calcium.** Calcium, a mineral, is important for a strong immune system because it helps your bones to grow and keeps them healthy. The amount of calcium absorbed by the bones during your teenage years will determine how strong your bones will be as an adult. A lack of calcium can cause brittle bones that have a tendency to fracture. It is also a common cause of a disease called osteoporosis, which often strikes older women. Osteoporosis causes the length and the density of bones to shrink, so that they become unable to support a person's weight. Calcium can be found in milk and other dairy products, in calcium-

fortified beverages such as soy milk and orange juice, and in dark green vegetables.

● **Healthy Foods.** Whole grains are better than products made with bleached (white) flour because they provide the body with complex carbohydrates for long-term energy, and because they contain fiber. Fiber does not get absorbed into the body; it passes through the digestive system easily. People who eat a high-fiber diet have a lowered risk for obesity, heart disease, and certain types of cancer. Fruits and vegetables, especially dark green, leafy vegetables, are also necessary for a healthy immune system. Many vegetables and fruits are high in essential vitamins A and C, and they are naturally low in fat. Fruits are best when eaten fresh (as opposed to canned or dried); likewise, fresh, raw vegetables have more vitamins than frozen ones.

● **Water.** Don't forget to drink plenty of water. Medical experts recommend drinking at least eight glasses of water per day. Water helps to flush toxins out of your system and keeps all of your internal organs hydrated.

Bad Things

● **Sugar.** A moderate amount of sugar won't hurt most people, but it is definitely a good idea to avoid consuming too much of it. The sugar in just one can of soda can dramatically elevate insulin levels and depress immune function by up to 50 percent for more than five hours! Sugar also blocks the body's ability to absorb Vitamin C. Instead of consuming sugary soft drinks or candy, try

eating healthy snacks, such as fruit, whole-grain bagels or crackers, hummus, sesame bars, popcorn, sorbet, nuts, and unsweetened fruit juice.

- **Fat.** A diet heavy in saturated fats, such as those found in beef or butter, can cause a deadly buildup of artery-clogging plaque. A high-fat diet can also lead to weight gain. Staying at a healthy weight is important because obesity—weighing 20 percent more than your recommended weight—decreases your immune strength considerably. Extra weight causes a person's heart to work overtime to perform its regular functions.

- **Caffeine.** Caffeine is a drug that increases the heart rate. It can make you edgy, nervous, and irritable. Many people rely on caffeinated beverages, such as coffee or soda, to keep alert during the day. This is a dangerous habit. Try to limit your consumption of caffeinated drinks to a cup a day—or, better yet, none at all. Get the proper amount of rest and sleep that you need instead of using caffeinated products to wake you up. Remember that caffeine can also be found in products such as chocolate and over-the-counter medications.

- **Tobacco.** Each year, almost 400,000 Americans die prematurely from the effects of smoking. Smoking seriously endangers your health, and the toll that it takes on the immune system is dramatic. It accounts for the vast majority of lung cancer deaths, and is also the leading cause of emphysema (a lung disease), chronic bronchitis, and atherosclerosis, which is a buildup of plaque in the arteries that can lead to heart attack or stroke.

The photo above shows a cancerous human lung. Smoking causes the vast majority of lung cancer deaths.

● **Alcohol.** Alcohol is a toxic drug that many people first begin to experiment with while they are teenagers. Regular, long-term alcohol consumption has serious damaging effects on the body's internal organs, especially the liver and spleen. Alcohol abuse also causes insomnia, short-term memory loss, and gastrointestinal problems such as pancreatitis, which is an inflammation of the organ responsible for digestion. Alcohol is high in calories, but offers no nutritional value.

Vitamins and Supplements

While taking vitamins that contain certain nutrients isn't harmful, most doctors and nutritionists believe that it is better to get vitamins directly from a food source. In other words, it is better to eat an orange for a daily dose of Vitamin C than it is to get it in pill form. It doesn't hurt to take a daily multivitamin for nutritional backup, but try to obtain most of your vitamins through your dietary choices. If you have questions about what is good to eat and what isn't, consult your doctor, and take a look at the For More Information and For

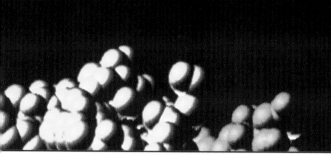

Further Reading sections at the back of this book.

Stress and the Immune System

Stress is unavoidable. Everyone experiences stress—little things such as waiting on line or bickering with friends, or, sometimes, traumatic experiences such as a loved one's death. It is important to develop healthy coping strategies for stressful situations, because an inability

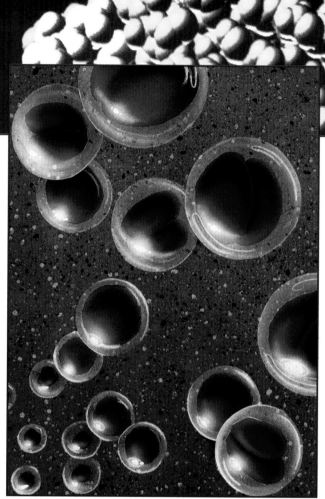

Stress can cause abnormal cell division of B cells and T cells, leading to immune suppression.

to handle stress takes its toll on the immune system, weakening it and leaving you at risk for disease. If stress is not dealt with, it can cause emotional problems such as depression, anxiety, and anger. It can also lead to physical problems such as lack of concentration, fatigue, and drug and alcohol abuse.

There are two main types of stress: acute and chronic. Acute stress is the result of a sudden or uncontrollable thing, such as an unexpected loud noise, a natural disaster, or a surgical operation. Chronic stress, on the other hand, is daily or ongoing. It includes such things as a regular lack of sleep, long-term physical pain, and day-to-day hassles such as traffic jams or a difficult job.

An upset stomach can be a symptom of stress.

Medical studies have proven that psychological stressors can cause a kind of cell division among T cells that hinders healthy immune function. While the cell division was most dramatic among the people in the study who reacted badly to stress (as opposed to the people who dealt with stress well), the results show that stress and immune suppression are linked. Finding out that you have a disease can be frightening and will certainly cause you stress, but many illnesses, such as cancer, are thought to be affected by the accumulation of stress. In other words, extra stress can worsen the symptoms of illness; therefore it is even more important for sick people to find ways to cope.

The physical signs of stress are not always easy to notice at first. Many people are not in touch with their emotional reactions and only realize that they are troubled once stress has taken a physical toll. If you are suffering from frequent headaches, insomnia (inability to sleep), upset stomach, fatigue, or other health problems, it may be due to an increase in stress in your life. Stress can also show itself through emotional symptoms, such as increased irritability, anxiety, sadness, or anger.

Healthy Ways to Deal with Stress

While it is impossible to eliminate all stress from your life, the good news is that most symptoms of stress can be greatly reduced. Here are some steps to take in managing your stress.

● Try to be aware of your own personal "triggers" for stress. Not everyone reacts to the same events with the same level of stress. For instance, you may hate having a jam-packed schedule, while your best friend thrives at a hectic pace and may actually find a lack of activity to be stressful. Recognizing your personal stress triggers is a first step toward dealing with them, because it helps you to feel more in control.

● Be more self-tolerant. This means giving yourself a break, and understanding that change, losses, and disappointments are a part of everyone's life. There are many situations over which a person has little or no control, such as the death of a pet or being laid off from a job. Often, people in these situations blame themselves for what has happened. But it really doesn't help the situation or one's level of stress to be angry or overly self-critical. Keep problems in perspective, and remember that bad things happen to everyone sometimes.

● Whenever possible, tackle stress head-on. Denial and procrastination, or putting things off, are two classic forms of avoiding stress that only create more stress in the long run. If you are upset with someone, don't brood—find the person and try to talk it out. If you

are having difficulty with a subject or project at school, seek out support from your teachers. Try not to avoid or distract yourself from your problems, and don't be afraid to ask friends, parents, and teachers for help.

● Figure out what makes you feel better in times of stress. Exercise is a great stress reliever. Regular exercise allows the body to produce natural chemicals, called endorphins, that aid in relaxation, antigen-fighting, and healthy blood flow. Meditation and yoga are very popular and effective ways to cope with the pressures of daily life. It is also important not to isolate yourself from others, so spend time with friends and family. And get enough sleep. Deep sleep allows the body's antigen fighters to do their work.

● If you feel seriously unable to cope with certain situations in your life, it is important to seek professional help as soon as possible. Talk to a counselor, psychologist, or other trusted adult who can get you the help that you need.

Conclusion

It is important to keep your immune system healthy and strong. When you are in good physical and emotional condition, you have the ability to fight off infections. You will also look and feel great and have energy to burn. Practice preventive medicine and keep your immune system—and yourself—in the best shape possible.

Glossary

acute stress
The result of sudden and/or uncontrollable problems that can take an emotional, physical, or mental toll on one's well-being.

antibiotic
Chemical substance such as penicillin that destroys infected cells without harming uninfected ones.

antigen
Toxic substance, such as bacteria or a virus, that attacks the body and stimulates an immune response.

atherosclerosis
A buildup of plaque in the arteries that can lead to heart attack or stroke.

B cells
Cells that produce antibodies for an immune system response.

benign tumor
Noncancerous tumor that usually does not grow back once removed.

chronic stress
The result of daily or ongoing problems or hassles that can cause physical problems and emotional disturbances.

dendritic cells
Cells that migrate through the blood, acting as carriers to bring antigens to the spleen, where the appropriate B cells or T cells begin an immune response.

endorphins
Chemicals released naturally by the brain, especially after exercising, that produce a relaxed, happy feeling.

homeopathic
Related to the medical practice that treats disease by giving people a very diluted dose of the antigen that causes the disease.

immunization
When a person is given a vaccine that stimulates the immune system and produces immunity to a specific disease.

insulin
A hormone secreted by the pancreas that helps to regulate the body's blood sugar levels.

leukocytes
The family of white blood cells.

macrophages
Cells that travel through the blood to bring antigens to the spleen, where an immune response begins.

malignant tumor
Tumor, resulting from metastasis, that is cancerous.

metastasis
The growth of abnormal cells in the body that causes cancer.

mutate
To change in form.

osteoporosis
A bone disease, caused in part by a lack of calcium in the diet, which causes the bones to lose density and thereby become brittle.

parasite
An organism that lives off of another organism.

pathogenic
Something that causes disease.

T cells
Cells responsible for fighting disease in the immune system.

vaccine
A weakened form of a disease, usually given by injection, that helps to kill the disease-causing organisms by starting an immune response.

For More Information

In the United States

Centers for Disease Control and Prevention (CDC)
1600 Clifton Road, MS D-25
Atlanta, GA 30333
(404) 639-3534
(800) 311-3435
Web site: http://www.cdc.gov

National Institute of Allergies and Infectious Diseases (NIAID)
Office of Communications and Public Liaison
Building 31, Room 7A-50
31 Center Drive MSC 2520
Bethesda, MD 20892-2520
Web site: http://www.niaid.nih.gov

National Institutes of Health (NIH)
Visitor Information Center
Bethesda, MD 20892

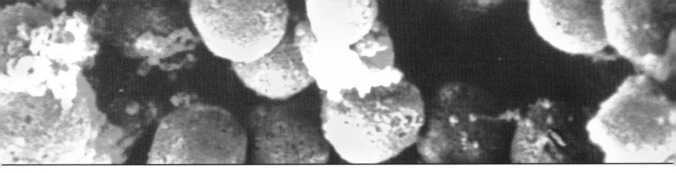

(301) 496-1776
Web site: http://www.nih.gov

In Canada

Laboratory Centre for Disease Control
Health Canada Bureau of Infectious Diseases
Tunney's Pasture
Ottawa, ON K1A 0L2
Web site: http://hwcweb.hwc.ca/hpb/lcdc/index.html

Web Sites

Dietsite
http://www.dietsite.com

Healthwell
http://www.healthwell.com

How Stuff Works
http://www.howstuffworks.com/immune-system.htm

Keep Hope Alive
http://www.execpc.com/~keephope/keephope.html

KidsHealth
http://www.kidshealth.org

World Health Organization (WHO)
http://www.who.int

For Further Reading

Feinstein, Alice, ed. *Prevention's Healing With Vitamins: The Most Effective Vitamin and Mineral Treatments for Everyday Health Problems and Serious Disease*. Emmaus, PA: Rodale Press, 1998.

Isler, Charlotte. *The Watts Teen Health Dictionary*. Danbury, CT: Franklin Watts, 1995.

Levinson, David, and Laura Gaccione. *Health and Illness: A Cross-Cultural Encyclopedia*. Santa Barbara, CA: ABC-CLIO, 1996.

Powell, Don R. *The American Institute of Preventive Medicine's Self-Care: Your Family Guide to Symptoms and How to Treat Them*. Allentown, PA: People's Medical Society, 1996.

Prevention Health Books Editors. *The Doctors Book of Home Remedies for Preventing Disease: Tips and Techniques So Powerful They Stop Diseases Before They Start*. Emmaus, PA: Rodale Press, 1999.

Salter, Charles A. *The Nutrition-Fitness Link: How Diet Can Help Your Body and Mind*. Brookfield, CT: Millbrook Press, Inc., 1993.

Ullman, Robert, and Judith Reichenberg-Ullman. *Homeopathic Self-Care: The Quick and Easy Guide for the Whole Family*. Rocklin, CA: Prima Publishing, 1996.

Index

Credits

About the Author

Susie Derkins is a poet and dressmaker who lives in New York City's East Village.

Photo Credits

P. 7 © Secchi, Lecaque, Roussel, UCLAF, CNRI/Science Photo Library (SPL)/Photo Researchers, Inc.; p. 8 © Life Art; p. 9 © Prof. P. Motta/Dept. of Anatomy/University "La Sapienza," Rome/SPL/Photo Researchers, Inc.; p. 10 © Alfred Pasieka/SPL/Photo Researchers, Inc.; p. 11 © John Bavosi/SPL/Photo Researchers, Inc.; p. 13 © Custom Medical; p. 14 © SPL/Custom Medical; p. 17 © Biophoto Associates/Photo Researchers, Inc.; p. 18 © Dee Breger/Photo Researchers, Inc.; p. 19 © Dr. Gopal Murti/SPL/Custom Medical; p. 20 © Robert Becker, Ph.D./Custom Medical; p. 21 © F. Wyda/Custom Medical; p. 22 © Life Art; p. 23 © Professors P.M. Motta, G. Macchiarelli, S.A. Nottola/SPL/Photo Researchers, Inc.; p. 25 © Alfred Pasieka/SPL/Photo Researchers, Inc.; p. 27 © Secchi-Lecaque/Roussel-UCLAF/CNRI/SPL/Photo Researchers, Inc.; p. 29 © Nancy Kedersha/Immunogen/SPL/ Photo Researchers, Inc.; p. 33 © Custom Medical; p. 36 © SPL/Custom Medical; p. 37 © Bryson Biomedical Illustrations/Custom Medical; p. 38 © Life Art.

Cover, front matter and back matter © SPL/Custom Medical: thymus with T lymphocytes. Cover illustration © Life Art. Intro background © Robert Becker, Ph.D./Custom Medical: mammalian bone marrow.
Ch.1 © Michael Abbey/Photo Researchers, Inc.: thymus.
Ch. 2 © Dr. R. Dourmashkin/SPL/Custom Medical: Asian flu virus.
Ch. 3 © Keith Porter/Photo Researchers, Inc.: daughter cells of recent cell division, still joined by a slender strand.
Ch. 4 © Oxford Molecular Biophysics Laboratory/SPL/Photo Researchers, Inc.: computer graphic of antibody-antigen complex.

Layout

Geri Giordano

Series Design

Cindy Williamson